Pressure Cooker Recipes:
Are You Busy? 65 Fast and Easy Pressure Cooking Ideas to Prepare Scrumptious Meals in No Time!

Copyright © 2014 by Annette Goodman

Contents

My Mailing list: If you would like to **receive new Kindle reads** on **weight loss, wellness, diets, recipes and healthy living** for **FREE** I invite you to my Mailing List. Whenever my new book is out, I set the free period for two days. You will get an e-mail notification and will **be the first to get the book for $0** during its limited promotion.

Why would I do this when it took me countless hours to write these e-books?

First of all, that's my way of saying **"thank you"** to my new readers. Second of all – **I want to spread the word about my new books and ideas.** Mind you that **I hate spam and e-mails that come too frequently** - no worries about that.

If you think that's a good idea and are in, just follow this link:
http://eepurl.com/6elQD

Introduction

Hello Friends!
Thanks for choosing this cookbook!

My name is Annette and I'm a huge wellness lifestyle aficionado... but also a working mum. Although my diet is gluten-free (I'm coeliac) and often vegan, I'm married with kids. I do everything to provide them with varied and delicious diet. This is my first book which aims at **"regular"**, **everyday recipes for busy people who don't follow any diet in particular.** Since you don't have too many time on your hands when you're working 9-5 and also maintaining your own diet, this book's focus is on **pressure cooker recipes.** This sweet little device will allow you to **prepare delicious and healthy meals in no time** – although slow cooker is nice to have, pressure cooker is something I definitely couldn't live without.

Majority of meals in this book can be prepared in under 20 minutes – there's pork, beef, poultry, fish, seafood, soups, sauces, bouillons, desserts and vegetable meals – all these scrumptious eats of my choosing that my family loves and keeps asking for!

Enjoy! : -)

Section 1: Beef, Pork and other Meats

Spicy Ribs in Sauce
Serves: 4
Cooking time: 30 minutes

Ingredients:

- 3 cups ketchup
- 3 tbsp. red wine
- 2 tbsp. Worcestershire sauce
- 1 tbsp. brown sugar
- 1 teaspoon mustard
- 2 teaspoons chili powder
- 1 teaspoon salt
- 1 teaspoon pepper
- 2.65 lbs. (1.2 kg) ribs with the fat cut off
- 2 tbsp. vegetable oil
- 1 large onion, chopped
- 1 cup water
- 1 tbsp. flour

Directions:

1. In a bowl, thoroughly combine all of the ingredients except the ribs, oil, onion, water, and flour.
2. Add the ribs, stir thoroughly, and marinate in the fridge for 4 hours.
3. Divide the ribs into 2 portions and save the marinade for later. Heat the oil in the fast cooker for about 2 minutes; fry the beef in batches from all sides.

4. With the remaining oil after frying, add onions, and then fry it and stir it constantly until browned.
5. Add ribs, marinade, 1-cup of water, and mix. Close the pressure cooker; bring to a full power using high heat.
6. Reduce the heat and cook for 30 minutes. Remove them from heat and put them aside to cool.
7. Open the pressure cooker, arrange the ribs on plates, (keep them warm) and remove all of the grease from the cooker.
8. In a separate bowl, gradually add the remaining water (1 cup) to flour, while stirring the flour constantly to get a smooth mixture.
9. Gradually add the mixture of flour and water to the remaining fluid from the pressure cooker and stir constantly using a whisk.
10. Put the pressure cooker on medium heat and cook until the sauce for about 3 minutes and stir it constantly.
11. Pour the ribs with the sauce and serve warm.

Chilli Con Carne

Cooking time: 18 minutes

Serves: 10

Ingredients:

- 2.2 lbs. (1 kg) lean ground beef
- 1 cup olive oil
- 2 large onion, chopped
- 6 cloves garlic, finely chopped
- 1 cup red beans, soaked
- 4 large tomatoes (peeled and sliced) or 3 cups canned tomatoes (drained and sliced) + 1 tbsp. tomato passata
- 2 bay leaves
- 1 tbsp. salt
- 3 tbsp. chilli powder
- 1 teaspoon pepper
- 1 teaspoon dried basil
- 2 teaspoons ground cumin
- 2 cups water

Directions:

1. Divide the meat into two portions. Heat 2 tbsp. of oil in the pressure cooker. Sauté the first portion and remove it from the pressure cooker. Add another 2 tbsp. of oil, sauté, and remove the second portion.
2. Pour the remaining oil (4 tbsp.); add onion and garlic to the pressure cooker. Fry and stir it constantly until the onion is browned.

3. Add meat and all of the remaining ingredients to the pressure cooker and stir.
4. Close the pressure cooker and bring it to full pressure on high heat.
5. Reduce the heat and cook for 18 minutes.
6. Remove the pressure cooker from the heat and leave to cool slowly.
7. Open the pressure cooker and remove the bay leaves. Serve warm.

Marinated Beef Roast
Serves: 6

Cooking time: 45 minutes

Ingredients:

- 3 lbs. (1.4 kg) rump of beef, boneless
- 1 cup white wine vinegar
- 1 large onion, chopped
- 1 cup water
- 1 clove garlic
- 1 bay leaf
- 7 grains of pepper
- 3 cloves
- 1 tbsp. sugar
- 1 teaspoon salt
- 1 lemon, sliced
- 1 tbsp. rapeseed oil (canola oil, but you can also use sunflower oil)
- 6 gingerbread cookies, crumbled

When reducing the number of servings, do not reduce the amount of marinade.

Directions:

1. Put the meat into a large bowl (glass or ceramic). In the saucepan, mix all the remaining ingredients except lemon slices, oil, and gingerbread.

2. Bring the mixture to a boil over high heat, pour the meat with it, and add lemon slices.
3. Cover the bowl and marinate in the fridge for 2 days, turning the meat once or twice a day.
4. Remove the meat from the marinade and dry it thoroughly with paper towels. Measure out one-cup of marinade and save it for later.
5. Heat oil in the pressure cooker for about 1 minute. Add meat; fry it on both sides until golden browned, and then remove it.
6. Pour 1 cup of the preserved marinade in the pressure cooker, and put the meat on the perforated inset.
7. Close the pressure cooker by bring to full power using high heat. Then reduce the heat and cook for about 45 minutes.
8. Remove the pressure cooker from the heat and leave to cool slowly.
9. Open the pressure cooker, arrange the meat on the plates, and remove the inset.
10. Place the pressure cooker over medium heat, add the gingerbread cookies, and cook until the sauce thickens, stirring constantly.
11. Serve warm, poured with the sauce.

Beef Roast in Vegetables
Serves: 6

Cooking time: 37 minutes

Ingredients:

- 2.42 lbs. (1.1 kg) rump of beef, boneless
- 2 cloves of garlic, minced
- 1 teaspoon salt
- 1 teaspoon pepper
- 1 tbsp. flour
- 2 tbsp. rapeseed oil (canola oil, but you can also use sunflower oil)
- 3 cups natural lean beef broth
- 1 glass dry red wine
- 1 small (4.2 oz., 120 g) carrot, chopped
- 1 stalk of chopped celery
- 1 medium (5.3 oz., 150 g) turnip, peeled and cut into slices
- 1 small (2.65 oz., 75 g) green pepper, seeded and chopped
- 1 small (2.1oz., 60g) onion with 4 cloves impinged
- 1 large (6.35 oz., 180 g) onion, coarsely chopped

When reducing the number of servings, do not reduce the amount of broth and wine.

Directions:

1. Rub the meat with garlic, salt, and pepper, and dredge the meat in flour on all sides.
2. Heat the oil in the pressure cooker for 2 minutes.

3. Add the meat, fry from both sides until slightly-golden brown.
4. Remove the pressure cooker from the heat, add broth, and stir.
5. Arrange the remaining ingredients around the meat. Close the pressure cooker; bring to full power over high heat.
6. Reduce heat and cook for 37 minutes.
7. Remove the pressure cooker from the heat and leave to cool slowly.
8. Open the pressure cooker; arrange the meat on plates.
9. Strain the remaining liquid after cooking and pour it in the pressure cooker.
10. Place the pressure cooker over high heat and cook until you reduce the volume by half; stirring occasionally reduces the volume of the liquid.
11. Serve the roast warm with sauce.

Pork and Beans Rural Style
Serves: 4

Cooking time: 40 minutes

Ingredients:

- 14 oz. (400 g) sweet white runner beans, soaked overnight
- 7 oz. (200 g) smoked bacon, cut in bars or cubes
- 7 oz. (200 g) normal or dried sausage, sliced
- 1-2 tbsp. tomato puree
- 1 medium onion, peeled and cubed
- 1 tbsp. lard
- 1.5 tbsp. flour
- salt, pepper
- paprika
- ground cumin
- marjoram
- allspice, bay leaf

Directions:

1. In the pressure cooker, pour enough water to cover the beans and cook them until they are tender. It should take about 20-30 minutes on high power.
2. Once they are ready, remove the heat to low.
3. In the meantime, in the saucepan, fry the bacon and sausage. Do not use oil; bacon is fat enough.
4. Add onions and fry until it gets glassy.
5. Add onions and meat to the pressure cooker.

6. Simmer the beans, meat, and onion for 15 minutes until the aromas blend.
7. Add tomato puree and spices.
8. Mix lard, flour to a smooth mixture, and then add the mixture to the pressure cooker.
9. Cook for another 5-10 minutes until the whole meal thickens.
10. Serve with fresh bread cut in thick loafs.

Chow Mein
Serves: 3

Cooking time: 25 minutes

Ingredients:

- 7 oz. (200 g) chicken breast
- 7 oz. (200 g) noodles
- 7 oz. (200 g) cabbage, chopped
- 2.1 oz. (60 g) champignons, sliced
- 2 stalks of celery, cut into slices
- 2 eggs
- 2 teaspoons corn flour
- 1 garlic clove, minced
- 1 inch (2.5 cm) piece ginger, cut into slices
- 2 teaspoons soy sauce
- 2 teaspoons chili sauce
- 2 teaspoons tomato sauce
- 2 teaspoons vinegar
- 6 tbsp. peanut oil
- salt to taste

Directions:

1. Rinse the chicken and cook in the pressure cooker with 1-cup of water for 10 minutes.
2. Save the broth and cut the meat into stripes. Pour 3 cups water, add noodles, and salt.

3. Close the pressure cooker and bring it to its full power over high heat

4. Reduce the heat to medium and cook for 5 minutes.

5. Remove the pressure cooker from the heat and open immediately after to release the accumulated steam.

6. Pour the pasta with cold water; strain it and leave to cool. In a skillet, heat the 1-tablespoon of oil, pour the lightly beaten eggs, and stir-fry until dense. Cut the omelet into strips and remove from the pan.

7. Now heat two tbsps. of oil in the same saucepan and sauté garlic, leeks, cabbage, mushrooms, ginger and chicken.

8. Add ½ of cup of chicken broth mixed with soy sauce and corn flour.

9. Simmer until the sauce thickens. Add tomato sauce, chili sauce, and vinegar.

10. In a different saucepan, heat the cooked noodles of the remaining oil for 5 minutes.

11. Transfer to a platter and garnish with strips of omelet; pour with the sauce with chicken and vegetables and serve hot.

Canned Beef with Onion
Serves: 6

Cooking time: 1 hour

Ingredients:

- 2 cups water
- 2.9 lbs. (1.3 kg) canned beef
- 1 small (120 g) onion, finely chopped
- 4 cloves
- 6 grains coarsely ground pepper
- 1 bay leaf
- 1 clove garlic, minced

When changing the number of servings, do not change the amount of water.

Directions:

1. Put the meat and all of the ingredients in the pressure cooker and add water.
2. Close the pressure cooker and bring it to its full power over high heat.
3. Reduce heat and cook for 15 minutes.
4. Remove the pressure cooker from the heat and leave to cool slowly.
5. Open the pressure cooker, arrange the meat on the plates, and serve warm.

Grilled Shaslik Kebab with Fried Rice
(Grill Required)
Serves: 4

Cooking time: 30 minutes

Ingredients:

- 17.6 oz. (500 g) lamb, diced
- 8 oz. (225 g) rice
- 4 small onions, cut in halves
- 4 small tomatoes
- 1 large red bell pepper, cut into 12 slices in length
- 1 tbsp. vinegar
- 1 inch (2.5 cm) part of ginger root, grated
- 8 garlic cloves, minced
- 2 tbsp. rapeseed oil (canola oil, but you can also use sunflower oil)
- salt and pepper to taste

Directions:

1. Marinate the lamb in garlic, ginger, vinegar, and salt for 2 hours.
2. Rinse the rice, soak for half an hour in two cups of water and then drain.
3. Thread onion, tomato, pepper, and meat onto skewers; alternating as you want.
4. Smear with olive oil and place it on a hot grill, turning from time to time.
5. In the pressure cooker, heat the oil, put the rice in, and fry for a few minutes until it starts sticking to the bottom.

6. Pour 350 ml water, season with salt. Close the pressure cooker and bring it to its full power over high heat.
7. Reduce heat to medium and cook for 3 minutes.
8. Leave the pressure cooker to cool slowly and then open it.
9. Put the rice on plates and place the skewers on it.

Spring Meatballs
Serves: 6
Cooking time: 12 minutes

Ingredients:
- 1 lb. (450 g) lean ground beef
- 0.5 lb. (225 g) ground pork
- 2 slices of bread soaked in water and squeezed
- 2 eggs
- 1 small onion, finely chopped
- 1 teaspoon salt
- 1 teaspoon paprika
- 1 teaspoon grated lemon peel
- 1 teaspoon Worcestershire sauce
- 4 teaspoon freshly squeezed lemon juice
- 5 tbsp. chopped parsley
- 3 cups natural vegetable broth
- 6 tbsp. butter
- 6 tbsp. flour
- 2 tbsp. chive

When reducing number of servings, do not reduce the amount of broth during pressure-cooking. Amount of broth can be reduced proportionately when making a sauce.

Directions:

1. In a bowl, mix all the ingredients except ½ of the lemon juice (2 teaspoons), chives, broth, butter, and flour. Divide the mixture to 24 even portions and form balls of 4 cm diameter.
2. Pour the broth to the pressure cooker, bring it to a boil over high heat, and add the meatballs one by one.
3. Close the pressure cooker and bring it to its full power over high heat.
4. Reduce heat and cook for 3 minutes.
5. Remove the pressure cooker from the heat and leave to cool slowly. Open the pressure cooker, place the meatballs on plates, and keep warm.
6. Strain the remaining liquid after cooking and save it for later.
7. Melt the butter in the pressure cooker over a medium heat.
8. Add flour and cook over small heat while constantly stirring with the whisk for about 3 minutes.
9. Remove from the heat and gradually add the preserved liquid while sill stirring. Put the pressure cooker on medium heat.
10. Boil and stir constantly until sauce thickens (about 3 minutes).
11. Add remaining lemon juice and parsley while you are stirring.
12. Pour the meatballs with sauce and serve warm with rice or pasta.

Cooked Beef with Dumplings

Serves: 4

Cooking time: 20 minutes

Ingredients:

- 1.1 lbs. (500 g) beef silverside or loin (cut into 2 inch (5 cm) cubes)
- 2 large carrots, cut into strips
- 2 large onions, sliced
- 1 bay leaf
- salt and pepper to taste

Dumplings:

- 4.23 oz. (120 g) flour
- a pinch of baking powder
- 1 medium onion, chopped
- 1 tbsp. parsley, chopped
- salt and pepper to taste

Directions:

Dumplings:

1. Mix all the ingredients, add some cold water, and knead soft dough. Form 12 small balls.
2. Boil 6.8 fl. oz. of (200 ml) water in the pressure cooker and add the dumplings. Close the pressure cooker and bring it to its full power over high heat.

3. Reduce heat to a minimum and cook for 8 minutes. Open immediately after the release of steam, remove, and drain noodles.

Beef:

1. Pour 250 ml water in the pressure cooker. Add beef, onion, bay leaf, salt, and pepper. Close the pressure cooker and bring it to its full power over high heat.
2. Reduce heat to a medium heat and cook for 15 minutes. Leave the pressure cooker to cool slowly.
3. Once cooled, open and add carrots. Close the pressure cooker and bring it to its full power over high heat. Reduce heat to a minimum and cook for 3 minutes. Once again, leave the pressure cooker to cool slowly before opening.
4. Serve warm with dumplings.

Kheema Kebabs
Serves: 3
Cooking time: 20 minutes

Ingredients:

- 14.1 oz. (400 g) ground meat
- 2 tbsp. chickpeas
- 2 medium onions
- 1 inch (2,5 cm) piece of ginger
- 4 green chili peppers
- 2 red chili peppers
- 10 peppercorns
- 1 inch (2,5 cm) cinnamon pod
- 3 cloves
- 4 grains of cardamom
- a few leaves of coriander
- rapeseed oil (canola oil, but you can also use sunflower oil)
- salt

Directions:

1. Finely chop one onion, two green chilies, and coriander leaves.
2. Separately cut the remaining onions, green chilies, and gingers.
3. Put meat into the pressure cooker along with the onion and green chili with the ginger. Add red chili, peppercorns, cinnamon, cloves, coriander, and three cups of water.

4. Close the pressure cooker and bring it to its full power over high heat. Reduce heat to medium and cook for 7 minutes.

5. Remove the pressure cooker from the heat and immediately release the accumulated steam and open.

6. Add the chickpeas. Close the pressure cooker again and bring it to its full power over high heat.

7. Reduce heat to a medium and cook for 5 minutes.

8. Remove the pressure cooker from the heat and immediately release the accumulated steam and open; remove water if there is any left.

9. Mix all of the ingredients into a smooth paste. Once done, mix the paste with chopped onion, green chili, coriander, and salt.

10. Shape into flat patties and fry in deep oil.

11. Serve warm.

Ribs in Beer and Honey

Serves: 3

Cooking time: 25 minutes

Ingredients:

- 2. 9 lbs. (1.3 kg) ribs
- 2 tbsp. rapeseed oil (canola oil, but you can also use sunflower oil)
- 1 cup beer
- 1 cup honey
- 1 teaspoon mustard powder
- 1 teaspoon chili powder
- 1 teaspoon sage
- 1 teaspoon freshly squeezed lemon juice
- 2 teaspoons salt

Directions:

1. Divide the ribs into 3 parts. Heat oil in a pressure cooker for about 2 minutes, fry ribs in three batches on all sides.
2. Remove pressure cooker from the heat and remove the grease. Add ribs and the rest of ingredients while stirring thoroughly. Close the pressure cooker and bring it to its full power over high heat.
3. Reduce the heat to a medium heat and cook for 20 minutes.
4. Remove the pressure cooker from the heat and leave to cool slowly.
5. Open the pressure cooker, arrange the ribs on plates, or in bowls, and keep them warm.
6. Remove grease from the liquid that remained after cooking, put the pressure cooker on a medium heat and cook until the sauce's volume is reduced by half while stirring occasionally.

7. Pour the ribs with the sauce and serve warm.

Section 2: Fish and Seafood

Sweet and Sour Shrimps
Serves: 2
Cooking time: 10 minutes

Ingredients:
- 8.8 oz. (250 g) shrimps
- 4.4 oz. (125 g) cucumber, cut into diagonal strips
- 4.4 oz. (125 g) green beans, cut into diagonal strips
- 1 bunch of spring onions, cut into diagonal strips
- 3 medium peppers, cut into large pieces
- 2 medium carrots, cut into diagonal strips
- 1 stalk of celery, cut into diagonal strips
- 1 leek, cut into diagonal strips
- 2 cups peanut oil
- salt

Sauce:
- 1 cup vinegar
- 4 teaspoons honey
- 4 teaspoons soy sauce
- 6 drops tomato sauce
- 2 tbsp. cornstarch
- 1 teaspoon sugar

Dough:
- 2 eggs
- 1 teaspoon baking powder
- 2 tbsp. flour
- 1 cup milk

Directions:

1. In the pressure cooker, pour a glass of water and add the cleaned shrimps.
2. Close the pressure cooker and bring it to its full pressure on high heat. Reduce heat to medium and cook for 5 minutes.
3. Remove the pressure cooker from the heat and open immediately once the steam is released.
4. Remove and thoroughly drain the shrimps.
5. Prepare the dough: beat the eggs, then add flour, and milk alternately. Finally, add salt, baking powder, and a little water so there is enough to get thick, batter-like dough.
6. In a saucepan, heat the oil, dip shrimps in batter and fry in deep fat until they are golden and crispy.
7. Remove the shrimp and stir-fry in vegetables sequentially, drying them on a paper towel.
8. In a skillet, mix corn flour, salt, sugar, vinegar, honey, soy sauce, and tomato sauce. Add the vegetables and shrimp; bring to boil and then heat for 3 minutes.
9. Serve warm.

Fish Packets
Serves: 3
Cooking time: 10 minutes

Ingredients:

- 6 (16 oz., 450 g) Sole fillets
- 2 tbsp. lemon juice
- 1 teaspoon pepper
- 1 teaspoon salt
- 3 tbsp. butter
- 1 small (4.2 oz., 120 g) onion, finely chopped
- 2 cloves garlic, finely chopped
- 1 cup celery, finely chopped
- 3 cups (4.2 oz., 120 g) champignons, thinly sliced
- 1 cup dry white wine
- 1 large (8 oz., 225 g) tomato, peeled and sliced
- 4 green olives, sliced
- 1 handful dill
- 1 teaspoon ground thyme
- 3 cups water

When reducing the number of servings, do not reduce the amount of water.

Directions:

1. Rub the fish with lemon juice, pepper, and ½ of the salt (1 teaspoon), marinate for one hour.
2. Melt butter on a saucepan; add onion, garlic, and celery. Stir-fry until onion gets slightly browned.

3. Add champignons and wine; cook until the wine evaporates, stirring occasionally.

4. Add tomato, olives, dill, and remaining salt (1 teaspoon). Cook until the fluid evaporates, stirring from time to time.

5. Place each fillet on a piece of baking paper or aluminum foil. Evenly spread the mixture on the prepared fish.

6. Wrap the paper around the fish and fold the top and sides to form packets. Pour water into the pressure cooker and put the inset.

7. Arrange fish packets on the inset. Close the pressure cooker and bring it to its full pressure on high heat. Reduce the heat and cook for 3 minutes. Remove the pressure cooker from the heat and release steam.

8. Open the pressure cooker and arrange the fish on the plates. Serve it warm.

Salmon Steaks
Serves: 4

Cooking time: 10 minutes

Ingredients:
- 1 medium onion, sliced into rings
- 2 (28.2 oz., 800 g) salmon steaks - about 1 inch (2,5 cm) thick
- 1 cup dry white wine
- 1 teaspoon salt
- 1/8 teaspoon pepper
- 1 lemon, sliced

When reducing the amount of servings, do not reduce the amount of wine.

Directions:
1. Put inset into the pressure cooker and arrange the onion on it.
2. Place the fish on the onion and drizzle with the white wine. Season the fish with salt and pepper; arrange lemon slices on the fish, but save four slices to decorate the plates.
3. Close the pressure cooker and bring it to its full pressure on high heat. Reduce the heat and cook for 6 minutes.
4. Remove the pressure cooker from the heat and release steam. Open the pressure cooker, arrange fish on the plates and remove onion and lemon. Serve warm and adorned with lemon slices.

Fish Steak with Mushrooms
Serves: 4

Cooking time: 10 minutes

Ingredients:

- 1 cups dry white wine
- 1 tbsp. white wine vinegar
- 3 tbsp. soy sauce
- 1 inch (2.5 cm) piece of freshly grated ginger
- 1 tbsp. sugar
- 1 teaspoon salt
- 2 large or 4 small (800 g), halibut steaks with a thickness of approx. 2.5 cm
- 1 cups champignons, thinly sliced
- 1 cups shallots with chives chopped diagonally
- Save 1 tbsp. chives to garnish the meal

When reducing the number of servings, do not reduce the amount of marinade.

1. In a shallow bowl, mix all ingredients except fish, mushrooms, and shallots.
2. Add fish steaks, dip them in the sauce, and marinate for 1 hour.
3. Insert the cartridge into the pressure cooker and place the fish on it.
4. Pour the marinade into the cooker, place the mushrooms and onions, but don't use one tablespoon so you can decorate the fish.

5. Close the pressure cooker and bring it to its full pressure on high heat. Reduce heat and cook for 6 minutes.

6. Remove the pressure cooker from the heat and release steam. Open the pressure cooker and arrange the fish and vegetables on a plate. Keep warm.

7. Remove the inset from the pressure cooker. Place the pressure cooker over high heat, and cook until the liquid is reduced to half, and stir from time to time. Once ready, pour the fish with the sauce.

8. Serve warm and garnished with shallot and chives.

Fish Broth
Serves: 5

Cooking time: 15 minutes

Ingredients:
- 2 tbsp. butter
- 1 small onion, chopped
- 1 small carrot, chopped
- ½ cup celery, chopped
- 23.8 oz. (675 g) bones and head of white non-greasy fish (gills removed)
- 1 teaspoon salt
- 4 grains of white pepper
- 1 sprig of parsley
- 1 bay leaf
- 1 teaspoon dried thyme
- 6 cups water

Directions:
1. Melt butter in a pressure cooker. Add onion, carrots, and celery. Stir-fry until onion gets glassy.
2. Add remaining ingredients and mix well. Close the pressure cooker and bring it to its full pressure on high heat.
3. Reduce heat and cook for 15 minutes. Remove the pressure cooker from the heat and leave to cool slowly.
4. Open the pressure cooker and strain the broth through a fine sieve.

Pasta and Shrimps Casserole

Serves: 4

Cooking time: 10 minutes

Ingredients:

- 17.6 oz. (500 g) shrimps, cleaned and peeled
- 3.5 oz. (100 g) noodles
- 1 small pepper, chopped
- 1 small onion, chopped
- 11 tbsp. flour
- 1 oz. (30 g) butter
- 1.8 oz. (50 g) cheese, grated
- 10 fl. oz. (300 m)l milk
- 6.8 fl. oz. (200 ml) court bouillon (page 108)
- Salt and pepper to taste

Directions:

1. Chopped peppers and onion sauté in a little butter.
2. Make white sauce (page 109) out of flour, butter, and milk.
3. In a pressure cooker, boil the noodles in 6.8 fl. oz. (200 ml) of hot salted water for 2 minutes.
4. Grease a mold. Pour the court bouillon to a pressure cooker and bring to the boil.
5. Add the shrimp and salt. Close the pressure cooker and bring it to its full pressure on high heat. Reduce heat to minimum and cook for 3 minutes.

6. Leave the pressure cooker to cool slowly before opening. Remove and drain shrimp. In the mold, arrange layers of shrimps alternated with pasta.

7. Pour white sauce; sprinkle it with pepper, onion, and cheese. Season and cover with greaseproof paper or baking paper.

8. Pour 6.8 fl. oz. (200 ml) water in the pressure cooker. Put the inset and place the mold on it. Bring to boil.

9. Close the pressure cooker and bring it to its full pressure on high heat. Reduce heat to medium and cook for 5 minutes.

10. Leave the pressure cooker to cool slowly.

Fish and Potato Casserole
Serves: 4

Cooking time: 15 minutes

Ingredients:

- 17.6 oz. (500 g) fish (preferably salmon), cleaned and cut into fillets
- 4 medium potatoes, peeled and cubed
- 2 medium tomatoes, peeled and sliced
- 1 small onion, chopped
- 1.8 oz. (50 g) butter
- 1 fl. oz. (30 ml) milk
- salt and pepper to taste

Directions:

1. Cook potatoes for about three minutes in 1.7 oz. (50 ml) boiling water.
2. Mash them into puree; add milk, and half the butter. Season and mix well.
3. Grease the mold. Pour 5 fl. oz. (150 ml) water into the pressure cooker, put the metal cooking inset at the bottom, arrange the fish on it, season with salt, and bring to boil.
4. Close the pressure cooker and bring it to its full pressure on high heat. Reduce heat to minimum and cook for 2 minutes.
5. Leave the pressure cooker to cool slowly. Remove the fish.
6. In the mold, place half of the potatoes, the top layer of the fish and a layer of tomatoes, sprinkle with onion, pepper, and salt.
7. Continue layering fish and vegetables until you fill three molds. Pour melted butter and cover with the rest of the potatoes.

8. Prick with a fork and cover with greased greaseproof paper or baking paper. Pour five fl. oz. (150 ml) into the pressure cooker. Put the metal inset inside, and place the mold on it, bring to boil.

9. Close the pressure cooker and bring it to its full pressure on high heat. Reduce heat to minimum and cook for 6 minutes.

10. Leave the pressure cooker to cool slowly and serve warm.

Fish Goulash

Serves: 3

Cooking time: 5 minutes

Ingredients:

- 17.6 oz. (500 g) fish (preferably salmon), cleaned and cut into slices
- 3 medium onion, sliced
- 2 medium tomatoes, sliced
- 4 green chili peppers, sliced lengthwise
- 1 inch (2.5 cm) ginger piece
- 1 coconut - wipe coconut flesh to shreds, make two solutions out of coconut milk: more condensed (2 fl. oz., 60 ml) and less condensed (10 fl. oz., 300 ml).
- 2 tbsp. vinegar
- a few curry leaves
- 4 cloves, crushed
- 2 red onions, finely chopped
- 2 tbsp. oil
- salt to taste

Directions:

1. In a pressure cooker, heat the tablespoon of oil. Sauté white onion, chili, and ginger.
2. On top place the fish pieces and curry leaves.
3. Add salt, tomatoes, vinegar, and thinner milk. Close the pressure cooker and bring it to its full pressure on high heat. Reduce heat to minimum and cook for 2 minutes.

4. Leave the pressure cooker to cool slowly. After opening, add the remaining milk.
5. In another skillet, brown the red onion with cloves and add to the stew.

Fish Casserole with Tomato Sauce
Serves: 3

Cooking time: 10 minutes

Ingredients:

- 17. 6 oz. (500 g) fish (preferably salmon), cleaned and sliced thinly
- 3 medium potatoes
- 1 oz. (30 g) butter
- 2 tbsp. flour
- 6 tbsp. tomato sauce
- 2 fl. oz. (60 ml) milk
- salt and pepper to taste

Directions:

1. Cook potatoes for 5 minutes in five fl. oz. (150 ml) of boiling water, peel and mash into puree, then mix with milk and butter.
2. Grease the mold. Pour five fl. oz. (150 ml) water into the pressure cooker. Put the inset, arrange fish on it, sprinkle with salt, and bring to boil.
3. Close the pressure cooker and bring it to its full pressure on high heat. Reduce heat to minimum and cook for three minutes. Leave the pressure cooker to cool slowly.
4. Open the pressure cooker and remove the fish, but leave water and inset inside.
5. Season the fish and mix with flour.
6. Put 1/3 potatoes into greased form, then a layer of fish, 2 tbsp. tomato sauce, then again a layer of potatoes, fish, and sauce.

7. Once done, mix the remaining potatoes with the rest of the sauce and lay on the top.

8. Prick with a fork and cover with baking paper.

9. Pour five fl. oz. (150 ml) water into the pressure cooker. Put the inset, put the mold on it and bring to boil.

10. Close the pressure cooker and bring it to its full pressure on high heat. Reduce heat to medium and cook for 5 minutes.

11. Leave the pressure cooker to cool slowly. Serve warm.

Spicy Braised Squids
Serves: 3
Cooking time: 20 minutes

Ingredients:

- 17.6 oz. (500 g) raw squid carcasses – blanched, skinned, rinsed, cut into small pieces
- ½ cup soy oil
- 1 bunch of chives
- 1 flat teaspoon of ginger
- 2 tbsp. soy sauce
- 1 flat tablespoon potato flour
- salt
- water
- Optionally: 2 tbsp. dry cherry
- salt and pepper to taste

Directions:

1. Preheat oil in a pressure cooker, then fry squids, add salt, chives, finely ground ginger, and possibly sherry.

2. Pour enough water to cover squids.

3. Close the pressure cooker and heat 10-15 minutes from the moment you cross the threshold of the internal pressure.

4. After this time, open the pressure cooker and thicken the sauce with flour blend with two tablespoons of cold water.

Paella

Serves: 5

Cooking time: 25 minutes

Ingredients:

- large pinch of saffron, soaked in 5 fl. oz. (150 ml) boiling water for 10 minutes
- oil in spray
- 1 onion, finely chopped
- 2 cloves garlic, finely chopped
- 4 tomatoes, coarsely chopped
- 1 red bell pepper and 1 orange pepper, chopped
- ½ tbsp. roasted pepper/paprika
- 1 tbsp. thyme
- 12.3 oz. (12.3 oz. (350 g) basmati rice
- 30 fl. oz. (900 ml) hot fish broth
- salt and freshly ground black pepper
- 3.5 oz. (100 g) peas, fresh or frozen
- 16 oz. (450 g) cooked, chilled seafood, e.g. prawns, mussels and squid, rinsed and drained
- A handful of fresh parsley, finely chopped
- 1 lemon, cut into 4 parts

Directions:

1. In a big, deep skillet sprayed with oil; add onion and fry for five minutes on minimum heat, until tender.

2. Add garlic and tomatoes, fry for another 5 minutes.

3. Add red and orange pepper, paprika, and thyme then add the rice and cook for 2 minutes. Mix the rice with vegetables.

4. Add saffron with liquid, half the broth, and season.

5. Bring to boil, reduce heat to a minimum, and cook for 10 minutes.

6. Slowly pour in the broth– you don't have to add it all.

7. Cover and cook over low heat for 5-10 minutes.

8. Mix with peas and seafood. If necessary, add more broth.

9. Cook for five minutes until the seafood and rice are hot and tender.

10. Sprinkle with parsley and serve with lemon pieces

Squids Stuffed with Fish
Serves: 5

Cooking time: 25 minutes

Ingredients:

- 17.6 oz. (500 g) small squid carcasses - blanched, skinned, rinsed
- 7 oz. (200 g) fish fillets, rinsed, sliced
- 1 onion, grated
- 1 robust loaf soaked in milk
- 1 egg yolk
- 1 tablespoon chopped parsley
- 4 cloves of garlic
- 1 stock cube
- 2 fl. oz. (60 ml) oil
- 1 cup dry white wine
- 1 cup water
- 1 tbsp. flavored olive oil (e.g. oregano and basil)
- 1 carrot
- salt and pepper to taste

Directions:

1. A few hours before cooking, marinate the squids with water diluted wine (as an alternative you can use the water + vinegar), oil, and grated carrots.

2. Add fish fillets to grated onion and soaked loaf. Mix with two cloves chopped garlic, parsley, egg yolk, salt, and pepper.

3. Mix well. Remove squids from the marinade, fill with the prepared stuffing, and fasten with pins.

4. Heat the oil in the pressure cooker, and brown the stuffed squids on it. Then pour in the marinade in which the squids were soaked, add two remaining garlic cloves (whole), and then season with salt and pepper.
5. Close the pressure cooker and cook for 15-20 minutes counting from the moment you cross the threshold of the internal pressure.
6. Once done, open the fast pressure cooker, pour the squids with flavored olive oil mixed with garlic cloves, and remove them from the pressure cooker.
7. Cook for about five minutes until the sauce evaporates.

Section 3: Poultry

Deliciously Browned Tarragon Chicken Legs
Serves: 3

Cooking time: 15 minutes

Ingredients:

- 2.2 lbs. (1 kg) chicken legs

Marinade:

- 2 tbsp. Worcester sauce
- 1 tbsp. herbal spice mix
- 1 tbsp. golden chicken seasoning
- 1 tbsp. dark soy sauce
- a handful of tarragon
- 1 tbsp. butter
- 1 teaspoon potato starch
- 0.5 cup 18% cream

Directions:

1. One day before cooking, mix all of the marinade ingredients. Thoroughly coat the chicken legs in the marinade and then leave in the fridge overnight.

2. Once marinated well, fry a few tarragon sprigs on olive oil then discard and put to pressure cooker. Fry chicken legs on the same oil until slightly golden browned. Leave the saucepan as is for the next step.

3. In a mortar, grand tarragon leaves with one teaspoon of salt and rub chicken legs with the mixture. Put chicken legs into pressure cooker.

4. Add ½ cup water to the saucepan that you fried the chicken with and heat for a while until the water absorbs the taste.

5. Pour the mixture from the saucepan to the pressure cooker, close it, bring to maximum heat, and cook for 10 minutes.

6. Wait until the steam comes out, remove chicken legs, pour the liquid from the pressure cooker through a sieve and add potato starch diluted in a little bit of water.

7. Add butter and cream to the sauce. Pour the sauce to the pressure cooker, add the chicken legs, and heat for a while until warm, remove from the pressure cooker, and serve.

Lentil and Turkey Meal
Serves: 3

Cooking time: 5 minutes

Ingredients:

- ½ cup red lentils (Egyptian – don't require soaking)
- 1 cup brown rice (or white rice)
- ½ green pepper
- ½ red bell pepper
- 17.6 oz. (500 g) turkey thigh, rinsed, drained, cut into strips
- 1 onion, chopped
- ½ leek, cut into long strips
- 1 stalk of celery
- a few champignons
- a piece of savoy cabbage or 2-3 leaves or (e.g. in the winter time) a package of your favorite frozen vegetables
- 2½ cup chicken broth
- 1 bay leaf
- salt , pepper , paprika to taste

Additionally:

- Béchamel - cheese sauce

Directions:

1. Season the turkey strip and gently sprinkle with flour.
2. Sauté on oil and preheat the pressure cooker with olive oil, add onions, and continue frying. Add rice and lentils and then all the remaining ingredients.

3. Once the ingredients start sticking to the cooker, pour in the chicken broth.
4. Close the pressure cooker and bring to boil. Reduce heat and cook for another 3 minutes. Then, dinner's ready, you can pour it with Béchamel-cheese sauce.

Murgh Musallam
Serves: 5

Cooking time: 15 minutes

Ingredients A:

- 26.5 oz. (750 g) chicken
- 1 glass of sour milk
- 2 inch (5 cm) piece of ginger
- 6 garlic cloves
- 2 green chilli peppers
- 1 teaspoon chilli powder
- 1 teaspoon garam masala powder
- large pinch of turmeric
- salt to taste

Ingredients B:

- 3 large onions
- 2 inch (5 cm) piece of ginger
- 6 garlic cloves
- 6 cloves
- 6 peppercorns
- 1 inch (2.5 cm) piece of cardamom
- 4 cardamom seeds
- 6 almonds
- 1 teaspoon cumin seeds
- 1 teaspoon coriander seeds
- 1 teaspoon garam masala powder
- 3 cups oil

Directions - Ingredients A:

1. Clean the chicken pieces and prick with a fork.
2. Grind all of the spices in a mortar and mix with sour milk. Rub the chicken with the mixture and put in the refrigerator for two-to-three hours.

Directions - Ingredients B:

1. In a dry saucepan, roast all the spices except ginger, chilies, and garam masala.
2. Sauté chopped onions and garlic in oil and then put them aside. Grind roasted spices, ginger, almonds, fried onions, and garlic into a paste.
3. Brown the chicken on the hot oil in the pressure cooker. Add the paste made from „B Ingredients" and fry constantly stirring for 2 minutes.
4. Add one-cup of water. Close the pressure cooker and bring it to its full power over high heat.
5. Reduce heat to medium and cook for 7 minutes. Remove pressure cooker from the heat and immediately release the accumulated steam.
6. Open and sprinkle with garam masala and chili. Serve warm.

Braised Duck
Serves: 4
Cooking time: 15 minutes

Ingredients:

- 35.2 oz. (1 kg) duck, with bones removed and sliced
- 1.8 oz. (50 g) butter
- 1 lemon
- 5 fl. oz. (150 ml) vegetable bouillon (page 110)
- 10 fl. oz. (300 ml) Worcestershire sauce
- 1 tbsp. rosemary

Directions:

1. In the pressure cooker, melt butter and sauté the duck until browned.
2. Add Worcestershire sauce, seasonings, and broth. Close the pressure cooker and bring it to its full power boiling over high heat. Reduce heat to medium and cook for 12 minutes.
3. Leave the pressure cooker to cool slowly. Open and serve them warm with slices of lemon.

Chicken in Lemon Sauce
Serves: 10

Cooking time: 15 minutes

Ingredients:

- 3.75 lbs. (1.7 kg) chicken, skinless
- 3 tbsp. lemon juice
- 1 tbsp. grated lemon peel
- 1 large onion, chopped
- 1 cup celery, chopped
- 2 teaspoons salt
- 1 teaspoon pepper
- 1 teaspoon dried thyme
- 3 cups thin chicken broth
- 2 tbsp. butter
- 3 tbsp. flour
- 1 tbsp. chopped parsley

Directions:

1. Rub chicken with two tbsps. of lemon juice and put aside for one hour.
2. Put the chicken, remaining lemon juice (1 tbsp.), and all of the remaining ingredient (except butter, flour and parsley) into the pressure cooker, and mix well.
3. Close the pressure cooker and bring it to its full power boiling over high heat. Reduce heat and cook for seven minutes. Remove the pressure cooker from the heat and leave to cool slowly.

4. Open the pressure cooker; put chicken on a plate, and keep it warm.
5. Strain the liquid that remained after cooking, remove the fat, and save the liquid.
6. Melt butter in a pressure cooker on medium heat. Add flour and cook over low heat while thoroughly stirring with whisk for about 3 minutes.
7. Remove from the heat and still stirring, while gradually adding the preserved liquid. Put the pressure cooker on medium heat.
8. Cook and stir until the sauce thickens (about 3 minutes). Pour the chicken with sauce. Serve warm and garnished with parsley.

Spanish Style Chicken

Serves: 9

Cooking time: 15 minutes

Ingredients:

- 2.8 lbs. (1.3 kg) chicken, skinless and sliced
- 2 tbsp. olive oil
- 1 tbsp. butter
- 2 tbsp. water
- 2 large onions, chopped
- 4 cloves garlic (grated)
- 1 medium (green pepper, seeded and finely chopped
- 4 large tomatoes, peeled and cubed
- 1 tbsp. Worcestershire sauce
- 3 teaspoon dried estragon
- 3 teaspoon pepper
- 2 teaspoons salt
- 3 cups champignons, sliced

Directions:

1. Divide chicken into three parts. Heat olive oil and butter in a pressure cooker for about two minutes; fry the chicken in three batches.
2. Remove the pressure cooker from the heat and rinse with water to remove residues after frying.
3. Put pressure cooker over a heat; add onion, garlic, and green pepper.

4. Stir-fry for about four minutes. Add chicken and the remaining ingredients, and stir. Close the pressure cooker and bring it to its full power boiling over high heat.

5. Reduce heat and cook for six minutes. Remove the pressure cooker from the heat and leave to cool slowly. Open the pressure cooker and put the chicken on a plate, and keep warm.

6. Put the pressure cooker back over the high heat and cook until there is half of the fluid left and stir from time to time. Pour the chicken with the sauce, serve warm.

French Style Chicken in Wine
Serves: 6

Cooking time: 15 minutes

Ingredients:

- 1 cup + 3 tbsp. flour
- 2.8 lbs. (1.3 kg) chicken, sliced
- 5 tbsp. butter
- 3.5 oz. (100 g) ham, cut into parts (about 0.2 inch (5 cm) each)
- 2 tbsp. water
- 1 teaspoon salt
- black pepper, to taste
- 6 small onions, peeled (e.g. shallots)
- 2 cloves garlic, finely chopped
- 1 teaspoon dried thyme
- 1 small bay leaf
- 3 cups (225 g) champignons, finely chopped
- 1 cup Burgundy wine
- 1 cup thin chicken broth
- 1 cup Cognac
- 1 tbsp. chopped parsley

Directions:

1. Add one-cup flour to a plastic bag. Throw a few pieces of chicken to the bag and shake the bag to toss them in flour. Proceed this way until all the chicken is dipped in flour.

2. Melt one tbsp. of butter in a pressure cooker. Add ham and fry until it is slightly browned. Remove from the pressure cooker and save for later.

3. Divide the chicken into three parts; melt two tbsps. of butter in a pressure cooker, and then fry the chicken into three batches.

4. Remove the pressure cooker from the heat and then rinse with water to remove residues after cooking.

5. Put pressure cooker on a heat; add the remaining ingredients except (cognac), parsley, the remaining butter (2 tbsp.), and flour (3 tbsp.). Stir thoroughly.

6. Close the pressure cooker and bring it to its full power boiling over high heat. Reduce heat and cook 6 minutes. Remove the pressure cooker from the heat and leave to cool slowly.

7. Open the pressure cooker, arrange the chicken on plate, and keep warm. From the liquid that remained after cooking, remove the fat, and save 1 cup.

8. Melt remaining butter (2 tbsp.) in a pressure cooker on a medium heat. Add the remaining flour (3 tbsp.), and cook over low heat, while still stirring with a whisk for about three minutes.

9. Remove from the heat and, while still stirring, gradually add the saved liquid. Put the pressure cooker over medium heat. Continue to stir, until the sauce thickens (usually about 3 minutes).

10. Heat cognac in a saucepan. Set it on fire; pour the burning cognac to the sauce.

11. Stir and pour the chicken with sauce. Serve warm and garnished with parsley.

Porto Chicken
Serves: 6

Cooking time: 20 minutes

Ingredients:
- 3.5 lbs. (1.6 kg) chicken
- 1 teaspoon salt
- 1 teaspoon pepper
- 3 tbsp. rapeseed oil (canola oil, but you can also use sunflower oil)
- 2 tbsp. water
- 2 medium onions, chopped
- 8 cloves garlic, thinely chopped
- 2 teaspoons dried basil
- 1 cup Port wine
- 1 cup ketchup
- 1 tbsp. chopped parsley

Directions:
1. Rub chicken with salt and pepper and then divide chicken into three parts.
2. Heat olive oil in a pressure cooker for three minutes; fry the chicken in three batches.
3. Remove the pressure cooker from the heat, rinse with water to remove residues after cooking.
4. Put the pressure cooker over a heat and add onions and garlic. Stir-fry for about two minutes.
5. Add chicken and the remaining ingredients (except 1 cup ketchup and parsley), while stirring.

6. Close the pressure cooker and bring it to its full power boiling over high heat.

7. Reduce heat and cook five minutes. Remove the pressure cooker from the heat and leave to cool slowly.

8. Open the pressure cooker; add the remaining ketchup (1 cup), and mix.

9. Serve warm with pasta and garnished with parsley.

Ginger Chicken
Serves: 2

Cooking time: 12 minutes

Ingredients:

- half of a (28.2 oz., 800 g) chicken, cut into two portions
- 1 inch (2.5 cm) piece of freshly ground ginger
- 1 garlic clove (grated)
- 1 cup soy sauce
- 1 cup dry Sherry
- 1 cup water
- 1 teaspoon salt
- 2 teaspoons black pepper
- 1 shallot with chives, peeled and sliced
- 1 lemon, cut into thin slices

When reducing the number of servings, do not reduce the amount of liquids.

Directions:

1. Rub the chicken with garlic and ginger.
2. Pour soy sauce, cherry, and water into pressure cooker, and then put the inset inside. Put the chicken on the inset and sprinkle with salt and pepper.
3. Arrange the onion and lemon slices on the chicken. Close the pressure cooker and bring it to its full power boiling over high heat.

4. Reduce heat and cook for 10 minutes. Remove the pressure cooker from the heat and leave to cool slowly.

5. Open the pressure cooker and arrange chicken on the plates. Remove the onion and lemon slices. Serve it warm.

Chicken Paella
Serves: 6

Cooking time: 30 minutes

Ingredients:
- 2 (23.6 oz., 670 g) chicken fillets, cut into 2 inch (5 cm) parts
- 3 tbsp. olive oil
- 1 large (4.2 oz., 120 g) dry chorizo sausage, sliced into 0.4 inch (1 cm) parts
- 1 small onion, chopped
- 1 cup shallots with chives, peeled and sliced
- 1 cup long grain rice
- 1 medium green pepper, seeded and coarsely chopped
- 1 tbsp. pepper powder
- 1 teaspoon salt
- 1 teaspoon pepper
- 12 (4.2 oz., 120 g) shrimps, cleaned
- 12 clams, rinsed and brushed
- 1 teaspoon ground saffron melted in 2 tbsp. chicken broth
- 1 cup thin chicken broth
- 2 tbsp. lemon juice
- 1 tbsp. chopped parsley

Directions:
1. Divide chicken into two portions then heat olive oil in a pressure cooker for about two minutes.

2. Fry the chicken from all sides in batches and when removing each batch onto paper towels to remove excess fat.
3. To the olive oil that remained in a pressure cooker, add sausage, onions, and shallot.
4. Stir-fry, until the onions are golden browned. Add rice and fry until the rise gets glassy (about 3 minutes).
5. Remove the pressure cooker from the heat; add chicken and all of the remaining ingredients except parsley and stir.
6. Close the pressure cooker and bring it to its full power boiling over high heat. Reduce the heat and cook for 18 minutes.
7. Remove the pressure cooker from the heat and leave to cool slowly for 5 minutes, then release the steam and open the pressure cooker.
8. Serve warm and garnish with parsley.

Curry Chicken

Serves: 6

Cooking time: 20 minutes

Ingredients:

- 1 medium chicken (about 4.4 lbs., 2 kg)
- 1 cup sour milk
- 3 medium onions, grated
- 2 medium tomatoes, sliced
- 1 inch (2.5 cm) piece ginger
- 15 cloves garlic
- 1 teaspoon chillli powder
- 1 teaspoon coriander and cumin powder
- 2 teaspoons turmeric
- 1 teaspoon garam masala powder
- 1 cup olive oil
- salt to the taste

Directions:

1. Divide the chicken into parts. In a bowl, grind garlic and ginger to a paste.
2. Preheat the olive oil in the pressure cooker and fry the onion until slightly browned; add garlic and ginger paste, tomatoes, and sour milk.
3. Fry until the fat separates, then add chicken, seasoning powder, and salt.
4. Fry the chicken until they are golden brown and add two cups water.

5. Close the pressure cooker and bring it to its full power boiling over high heat. Reduce the heat to medium and cook for 7 minutes.
6. Remove the pressure cooker from the heat and leave to cool slowly.

Marengo Chicken
Serves: 5

Cooking time: 20 minutes

Ingredients:

- 2.2 lbs. (1 kg) chicken
- 8 oz. (225 g) crayfish meat
- 1 oz. (30 g) shallots, sliced
- 2 medium tomatoes, blenched and sliced
- 1.8 oz. (50 g) champignons, sliced
- 4 eggs
- 10 fl. oz. (300 ml) jus-lie sauce (page 112)
- 1 oz. (30 g) butter
- 3 clove garlic, sliced
- 1 tbsp. olive oil
- a few sprigs of fresh parsley, salt and pepper to taste

Directions:

1. Divide the chicken into parts and then sprinkle with salt and pepper.
2. Pour 6.8 fl. oz. (200 ml) water into the pressure cooker, put the inset at the bottom, and arrange crayfish on it. Close the pressure cooker and bring it to its full power boiling over high heat.
3. Reduce the heat to medium and cook for three minutes. Remove the pressure cooker from the heat and leave to cool slowly.
4. Open, remove the crayfish, and remove the water. In the pressure cooker, heat olive oil and then fry the chicken until golden

browned. Add shallots, garlic, champignons, tomatoes, spices, and dark sauce.

5. Close the pressure cooker and bring it to its full power boiling over high heat. Reduce heat to medium and cook for 10 minutes.

6. Remove the pressure cooker from the heat and leave to cool slowly.

7. Open, put chicken on a flat dish, drizzle it with sauce. Garnish with crayfish, planted eggs, croutons, and sprinkle with parsley.

Pharaoh's Chicken
Serves: 5

Cooking time: 15 minutes

Ingredients:
- 2.2 lbs. (1 kg) chicken
- 2.1 oz. (60 g) champignons, cut into stripes
- 11.8 oz. (50 g) ham, cut into strips
- 2 medium onions, peeled and sliced
- 2 medium tomatoes, peeled and sliced
- 3 tbsp. olive oil
- 3 tbsp. turmeric
- 6.8 fl. oz. (200 ml) chicken broth
- salt and pepper to taste

Directions:
1. Divide the chicken into parts. In the pressure cooker, heat olive oil, and fry the chicken until slightly browned.
2. Add ham, onions, champignons, and tomatoes. Add broth and spices.
3. Close the pressure cooker and bring it to its full power boiling over high heat.
4. Reduce heat to medium and cook for 10 minutes.
5. Leave the pressure cooker to cool down slowly. Open and serve warm.

Scottish Chicken and Leek Soup
Serves: 4

Cooking time: 15 minutes

Ingredients:

- 28.2 oz. (800 g) chicken, sliced
- 4 leeks
- 1 oz. (30 g) butter
- 10 fl. oz. (300 ml) broth
- bouquet garni (a small tied bunch of parsley, bay leaf and thyme)
- salt and pepper to taste

Directions:

1. Cut white parts of leeks into thin strips (so called *julienne*).
2. Pour broth into the pressure cooker. Add chicken, bouquet garni, salt, and pepper.
3. Close the pressure cooker and bring it to its full power boiling over high heat.
4. Reduce the heat to a medium and cook for 10 minutes.
5. Leave the pressure cooker to cool down slowly.
6. Pour the broth along with chicken to another vessel.
7. In the pressure cooker, melt butter and sauté the leeks. Add broth, chicken, and season.
8. Close the pressure cooker again and bring to full power boiling over high heat.
9. Reduce heat to medium and cook for 1 minute.

10. Put the pressure cooker aside and let cool down.
11. Open, remove chicken, remove the bones, and cut meat into thin strips (julienne).
12. Put chicken strips on the bottom of vases or plates, pour with hot soup, and serve immediately.

Section 4: Vegetables

Palak Paneer

Serves: 2-3

Cooking time: 30 minutes

Ingredients:

- a handful of fenugreek, chopped
- 12.3 oz. (350 g) spinach, chopped
- 7 oz. (200 g) paneer cheese, cubed
- 1 medium onion, peeled and sliced
- 3 medium tomatoes, chopped
- 0.4 inch (1 cm) piece of ginger
- 5 cloves garlic
- 1 teaspoon chili powder
- 1 cup milk
- 1/2 cup oil
- salt to taste

Directions:

1. Lightly fry paneer cheese. Put spinach and fenugreek in the pressure cooker; add one-cup water.
2. Close the pressure cooker and bring it to its full power boiling over high heat.
3. Reduce heat to medium and cook for 7 minutes.
4. Remove the pressure cooker from the heat and immediately release the accumulated steam.
5. Drain the water and mix spinach with fenugreek.

6. In a saucepan, preheat olive oil and brown the onion. Add ginger, garlic, and tomatoes.

7. Fry a few minutes and add spinach. After several minutes add paneer, chili, salt, and mix thoroughly. At the end, pour one-cup of milk and simmer on a low heat for two minutes.

Chickpeas Stew
Serves: 8

Cooking time: 30 minutes

Ingredients:

- 2 cups water
- 2 cup soaked chickpeas
- 2 tbsp. olive oil
- 1 large onion, finely chopped
- 3 cloves garlic, finely chopped
- 3 large tomatoes, peeled and coarsely chopped
- 1 medium green pepper, seeded and sliced
- 2 teaspoons salt
- 1 teaspoon pepper
- 1 teaspoon dried tarragon
- 3 teaspoon dried basil
- 1 tbsp. parsley, chopped

When reducing the number of servings, do not reduce the amount of water.

Directions:

1. Pour water to the pressure cooker; add chickpeas.
2. Boil over high heat and remove the foam, if it appears.
3. Close the pressure cooker and bring it to its full power boiling over high heat.
4. Reduce heat and cook for 18 minutes.
5. Remove the pressure cooker from the heat and leave to cool slowly.

6. Open the pressure cooker, dry the chickpeas, and remove shells, which fell off during cooking.
7. Rinse the pressure cooker. Preheat oil for about two minutes.
8. Add onion, garlic, and stir-fry until the onions are brown.
9. Add tomatoes, cook for about three minutes, stirring from time to time.
10. Add chickpeas and all the remaining ingredients except for parsley and mix thoroughly.
11. Reduce the heat and cook on a low flame for about five minutes, while stirring from time to time.
12. Serve warm and garnish with parsley.

Vegetable Pot
Serves: 8

Cooking time: 20 minutes

Ingredients:

- 2 medium carrots, sliced into 0.2 inch (0.5 cm) thick strips
- 1 medium zucchini, sliced into 0.4 inch (1 cm) thick slices
- 1 large onion, finely chopped
- 1 medium green pepper, seeded, cut into 1 inch (2.5 cm) pieces
- 1 small turnip, peeled and cut into 0.4 inch (1 cm) cubes
- 2 medium tomatoes, peeled and cut in eights
- 1 small head of cauliflower, divided into 1 inch (2.5 cm) florets
- 1 small bay leaf
- 1 teaspoon salt
- a pinch of pepper
- 1 teaspoon dried thyme
- 1 teaspoon dried marjoram
- 2 tbsp. Worcestershire sauce
- 1 cup water
- 2 tbsp. chopped parsley

When reducing the number of servings, do not reduce the amount of water.

Directions:

1. Put all of the ingredients except for one tbsp. parsley into the pressure cooker and mix thoroughly.

2. Close the pressure cooker and bring it to its full power boiling over high heat.
3. Reduce heat and cook two minutes.
4. Remove the pressure cooker from the heat and release the steam.
5. Open the pressure cooker, remove the bay leaf, arrange the vegetables in bowls, and keep warm.
6. Place the pressure cooker over large heat and cook until half of the liquid is left, while occasionally stirring.
7. Pour the vegetables with the sauces and serve warm and garnish with parsley.

Stuffed Tomatoes
Serves: 4
Cooking time: 15 minutes

Ingredients:

- 4 medium (6.3 oz. 180 g) fresh and firm tomatoes
- 1 tbsp. butter
- 1 small onion, finely chopped
- 2 tbsp. celery, finely chopped
- 1 cup champignons, finely chopped
- 1 slice of bread, crumbled
- 1 cup lean cottage cheese
- 1 teaspoon salt
- 1 teaspoon pepper
- 1 teaspoon cumin
- 1 tbsp. parsley, chopped
- 1 cup water

When reducing the number of servings, do not reduce the amount of water.

Directions:

1. Place the tomatoes stem to bottom, cut the tip of each tomato, and put it aside.
2. Using a spoon, hollow the tomatoes and slice the pulp.
3. In a saucepan, melt butter; add onion and celery, and stir-fry until the onions gets glassy.
4. Add champignons and sliced tomato pulp.

5. Cook, until the liquid evaporates, stirring from time to time.
6. Add all the remaining ingredients except for water and continue to stir thoroughly.
7. Divide the filling into four portions, stuff the tomatoes, and cover with the cut-off tomato top.
8. Pour water to the pressure cooker, place the pressure cooker inset on the bottom and arrange stuffed tomatoes on it.
9. Close the pressure cooker and bring it to its full power, boiling over high heat.
10. Immediately remove the pressure cooker from the heat and reduce the pressure placing the pressure cooker in about 10 cm cold water in a bowl or sink for about one or two minutes.
11. Open the pressure cooker and serve warm.

Stuffed Green Peppers
Serves: 4

Cooking time: 15 minutes

Ingredients:

- 4 medium (720 g) green peppers
- 1 cup water

Vegetarian filling:

- 1 cup boiled long grain rice
- 1 small (60 g) onion, grated
- 3 tbsp. tomato, peeled and finely chopped
- 1 teaspoon salt
- 1 teaspoon pepper
- 2 cups cheddar cheese, grated

Or tuna filling:

- 1 cup boiled long grain rice
- 1 small (60 g) onion, grated
- 3 tbsp. corn grains, drained
- 1 cup (45 g) champignons, finely chopped
- 1 can tuna in pieces
- 1 teaspoon salt
- 1 teaspoon pepper
- 2 cups cheddar cheese, grated

Directions:

1. Cut a hole around the tail of each pepper and remove the seed core' gently remove the remaining seeds from inside the pepper.

2. Mix all the filling ingredients in a bowl (vegetarian or with tuna) except for one-cup cheese.
3. Divide the filling into four even portions; stuff each pepper with the filling, kneading it well.
4. Pour water to the pressure cooker, put the inset, and place the peppers on the inset.
5. Close the pressure cooker and bring it to its full power, boiling over high heat.
6. Reduce heat and cook for 1 minute.
7. Remove the pressure cooker from the heat, reduce the pressure placing the pressure cooker in about 10 cm cold water in a bowl or sink for about one or two minutes.
8. Open the pressure cooker, remove the peppers, and sprinkle their tops with remained cheese (1 cup).
9. Bake the peppers in the oven until cheese melts, and serve warm.

Veggie Pulao

Serves: 2

Cooking time: 5 minutes

Ingredients:

- 21.8 oz. (50 g) rice, rinsed, soaked for half an hour in water and drained
- 3.5 oz. (100 g) green peas
- 2 medium carrots, cut into 0.8 inch (2 cm) bars
- 1.8 oz. (50 g) green beans, cut into 0.8 inch (2 cm) bars
- 2 cinnamon pods
- 4 seeds cardamom
- 6 cloves
- 2 small bay leaves
- 1 teaspoon cumin seeds
- 3 tbsp. olive oil
- salt to taste

Directions:

1. In the pressure cooker, fry cinnamon, cardamom, cloves, bay leaves, and cumin on olive oil.
2. After a while, add vegetables and fry for two minutes.
3. Add rice and salt, fry for additional minute.
4. Pour in 10 fl. oz. (300 ml) water. Close the pressure cooker and bring it to its full power, boiling over high heat.
5. Reduce heat to minimum and cook for three minutes.
6. Remove the pressure cooker from the heat and leave to cool slowly. Open and serve warm.

Sambar
Serves: 3
Cooking time: 10 minutes

Ingredients:

- 21.8 oz. (50 g) eggplant (you can also use different vegetable instead), cut into longitudinal slices
- 11.8 oz. (50 g) tuvar dal (pea variety), rinsed
- 1 oz. (30 g) tamarind, soaked in 2 cups water
- 1 tbsp. mustard seeds
- 1 teaspoon turmeric
- 1 teaspoon fenugreek seeds
- a pinch of asafetida
- half a bunch of cilantro, chopped
- 1 teaspoon peanut oil
- salt to taste

Sambar:

- 1 coconut, grated
- 5 red chilli peppers
- 1 teaspoon fenugreek seeds
- 1 teaspoon coriander seeds
- 1 teaspoon peanut oil

Directions:

1. Preheat one teaspoon of peanut oil and toast the desiccated coconut, chili peppers, coriander, and fenugreek seeds until golden browned, and then grind them to a paste.

2. In the pressure cooker, boil four cups water and add tuvar dal.

3. Close the pressure cooker and bring it to its full power boiling over high heat. Reduce heat to medium and cook three minutes.

4. Remove the pressure cooker from the heat and leave to cool slowly. Open.

5. In a separate saucepan, boil water in which you soaked tamarind with eggplant, salt, turmeric, and sambar paste. Cook until the eggplant gets tender.

6. Add boiled tuvar dal peas and hold on low heat for 3 minutes.

7. Season with peanut oil, mustard seeds, asafetida, and coriander seeds. Serve sprinkled with coriander.

Corn Egg Soup
Serves: 3

Cooking time: 40 minutes

Ingredients:

- 4 young corn cobs
- 2 eggs, soaked in boiling water for a moment
- 1 stalk of chopped celery
- 1 medium red pepper, thinly sliced
- 2 tbsp. corn starch
- 1 teaspoon Worcestershire sauce
- 1 teaspoon peanut oil
- salt and pepper to taste
- Optionally use one teaspoon of monosodium glutamate to strengthen the flavor (if you're not allergic to it)

Directions:

1. Mix cornstarch in a little bit of water. In the pressure cooker, boil 500 ml of water; add corncobs, red pepper, celery, salt, and pepper.
2. Close the pressure cooker and bring it to its full power boiling over high heat. Reduce heat to medium and cook for 15 minutes.
3. Remove the pressure cooker from the heat and leave to cool slowly.
4. Open, strain the broth into a separate pot, cut off the corn grains from the cobs, add to the broth, and put on low fire.
5. Add and mix the cornstarch in water, Worcestershire sauce, peanut oil, and monosodium glutamate and stir thoroughly.
6. Cook on a low heat for 15 minutes, at the end, add two raw eggs, and beat them with fork.
7. Serve warm with soy and chili sauce.

Matar Paneer

Serves: 2

Cooking time: 10 minutes

Ingredients:

- 12.3 oz. (350 g) green peas
- 7 oz. (200 g) paneer cheese, cubed
- 2 medium onions, grated
- 2 medium tomatoes, chopped
- 1 inch (2.5 cm) piece of ginger, chopped
- 1 teaspoon chilli powder
- 1 teaspoon cumin and coriander powder
- a pinch of turmeric
- a few coriander leaves
- 4 tbsp. oil
- salt to taste

Directions:

1. In the saucepan, lightly fry the paneer cheese.
2. In the pressure cooker, preheat the oil and slightly brown the onion. Add ginger and one-cup water then add the tomatoes, spices, chili powder, and salt.
3. Fry until separation of fat. Add peas and fry for 2 minutes and then pour ½ cup water.
4. Close the pressure cooker and bring it to its full power boiling over high heat. Reduce heat to medium and cook for three minutes.
5. Remove the pressure cooker from the heat and immediately release the accumulated steam.
6. Open, add paneer cheese, and then cook for another 2 minutes.
7. Serve sprinkled with chopped coriander.

Aloo Matar Curry

Serves: 2

Cooking time: 10 minutes

Ingredients:

- 2 large potatoes, peeled and cubed
- 7 oz. (200 g) hulled peas
- 1 large onion, grated
- 1 large tomato, chopped
- 1 inch (2.5 cm) ginger piece, chopped
- 1 teaspoon chilli powder
- 1 teaspoon ground cumin and coriander
- a large pinch of turmeric
- 3 tbsp. oil
- salt to taste

Directions:

1. Preheat the oil in the pressure cooker. Fry the onions and ginger, add tomato, and after several minutes add peas, potatoes, spices, and salt.
2. Stir-fry for two minutes. Then add two cups water. Close the pressure cooker and bring it to its full power boiling over high heat.
3. Reduce heat to medium and cook three minutes. Remove the pressure cooker from the heat and leave to cool slowly.
4. Serve garnished with coriander leaves.

Dum Aloo

Serves: 3

Cooking time: 20 minutes

Ingredients:

- 22 oz. (600 g) very small potatoes
- 2 cup soured milk
- 2 inch (5 cm) ginger piece
- 10 cloves garlic
- 1 green chilli pepper
- 1 teaspoon chilli powder
- a large pinch of turmeric
- 1 teaspoon ground cumin and coriander
- oil
- salt and pepper to taste

Directions:

1. Bring two cups of water to boil in the pressure cooker and add the potatoes. Close the pressure cooker and bring it to its full power boiling over high heat.
2. Reduce heat to medium and cook for 5 minutes. Remove the pressure cooker from the heat and immediately release the accumulated steam.
3. Remove the potatoes, peel, and prick them.
4. In a saucepan, preheat large amount of oil and fry the potatoes until golden browned.
5. Remove potatoes from the saucepan and drain on a paper towel.
6. Grind or mix ginger, green pepper and garlic to a paste. Mix the paste with soured milk, potatoes, spices, salt, and pepper.

7. Preheat three tbsp. of oil, pour in potatoes mix and soured milk, fry until the separation of fat, then pour in 1 cup water, and simmer for ten-to-twelve minutes on low heat.

Section 5: Desserts

Chocolate Soufflé
Serves: 2
Cooking time: 20 minutes

Ingredients:

- 4 oz. (115 g) chocolate
- 5 fl. oz. (150 ml) milk
- 5 eggs
- 1 oz. (30 g) butter
- 2 tbsp. flour
- 1 teaspoon sugar powder
- 5 drops vanilla essence

Directions:

1. Grease a pudding mold. Break the chocolate and melt in boiling milk. Cool down.

2. In a saucepan melt the butter, add flour, and fry for a while.

3. Add milk with chocolate and stir; heat until it thickens.

4. Let it cool down a bit and start adding one yolk egg at a time.

5. Add vanilla essence and sugar. At the end, mix gently with rigidly beaten egg whites.

6. Transfer to a mold and cover with greased baking paper.

7. Pour 6.8 fl. oz. (200 ml) water into the pressure cooker, place the inset on the bottom, and put the mold on it.

8. Close the pressure cooker and bring it to its full power, boiling over high heat.

9. Reduce heat to low and cook for 15 minutes.

10. Remove the pressure cooker from the heat and leave to cool slowly.

11. Open the pressure cooker, remove the paper, put an inverted plate on the mold, turn it upside down, and shake gently to get the soufflé.

12. Enjoy!

Carrot Halva
Serves: 2

Cooking time: 5 minutes

Ingredients:

- 17.6 oz. (500 g) carrots, grated
- 7 oz. (200 g) khoya, condensed unsweetened milk (or alternatively ricotta)
- 4.4 oz. (125 g) sugar
- 10 almonds, peeled
- 1.8 oz. (50 g) ghee (clarified butter)
- 1 teaspoon cardamom powder

Directions:

1. Put a carrot to the pressure cooker. Close the pressure cooker and bring it to its full power boiling over high heat.
2. Open immediately after the release of the accumulated steam. Add khoya, ghee, *and sugar.*
3. Fry until carrots are slightly browned.
4. Serve sprinkled with chopped almonds and cardamom.

Lemon Crème

Serves: 1

Cooking time: 10 minutes

Ingredients:

- 1 cup milk
- 1 egg
- 1 tbsp. sugar
- 1 teaspoon grated lemon peel
- 1 teaspoon lemon juice
- a tiny pinch of salt
- 3 cups water

Directions:

1. Bring milk to a boil and cool down a bit.
2. In a bowl, whisk the egg lightly; add sugar, peel, and juice from lemon and salt.
3. Mix well and while stirring, slowly pour in milk.
4. Grease two heat-resistant molds with butter and pour the cream into them.
5. Cover tightly with aluminum foil.
6. Pour water into the pressure cooker, put the inset, and arrange the molds on it.
7. Close the pressure cooker and bring it to its full power, boiling over high heat. Reduce heat and cook for 5 minutes.
8. Remove from heat and place in cold water for one-to-two minutes.
9. Open pressure cooker, remove the molds, and remove the foil.
10. Put aside to cool down, and then put in the refrigerator.
11. Serve chilled.

Apple-Date Pudding
Serves: 3

Cooking time: 1 hour

Ingredients:

- 1 large apple, peeled and sliced
- 1 cup dates, chopped
- 1 cup walnuts, chopped
- 1 cup + 1 teaspoon sugar
- 3 cups flour
- 1 teaspoon baking powder
- 3 teaspoon baking soda
- 3 teaspoon salt
- 1 teaspoon blend of ground root spices (cinnamon, nutmeg, allspice in the basic version; expanded version additionally contains ginger, cloves, coriander seeds, cumin and cayenne pepper - spices must be grated into a powder)
- 1 teaspoon ground nutmeg
- 1 teaspoon ground cloves
- 1 teaspoon ground cinnamon
- 2 eggs
- 2 tbsp. oil
- 3 cups water

When reducing the number of servings, do not reduce the amount of water.

Directions:

1. Mix apples, dates, and nuts with 1 cup sugar. Sieve flour with baking soda, salt, spice blend, cinnamon, nutmeg and cloves, and add then to the fruits. Mix well.

2. In a separate bowl, beat the eggs with oil, add to the ingredients from point 1, and stir thoroughly.

3. Put the mixture to 33.8 oz. (1 l) mold greased with butter, sprinkle with remaining sugar, and cover tightly with aluminum foil.

4. Pour three cups water to the pressure cooker, put the inset on the bottom, and place the mold on it.

5. Close the pressure cooker, but do not put the vent weight.

6. Cook over high heat until the valve begins to emit steam.

7. Reduce heat and be sure that the steam is still escaping from the vent; cook for 15 minutes.

8. After this time, apply a weight valve and bring to full power boiling over high heat.

9. Reduce the heat and cook for 40 minutes. Remove the pressure cooker from the heat and leave to cool slowly.

10. Open the pressure cooker, remove the mold, and gently separate the pudding from the mold using a knife. Put an inverted plate on the mold, turn it upside down, and shake gently to get the pudding.

11. Serve either warm or chilled.

Simple Apple Dessert

Serves: 2

Cooking time: 5 minutes

Ingredients:

- 2 apples, peeled, with cores removed, cut into quarters
- 7 oz. (200 g) sugar

Directions:

1. Boil 6.8 fl. oz. (200 ml) water in the pressure cooker, add sugar, and boil for a while to get a syrup consistency.
2. Add apples. Close the pressure cooker and bring it to its full power, boiling over high heat.
3. Reduce heat to low and cook for one minute.
4. Remove the pressure cooker from the heat and leave to cool slowly.
5. Serve cold with sweet cream.

Caramel Crème

Serves: 2

Cooking time: 12 minutes

Ingredients:

- 10 fl. oz. (300 ml) milk
- 2 eggs
- 4 tbsp. sugar
- A pinch of nutmeg

Directions:

1. In a thick bottom pan, boil heaped tbsp. sugar melted in a little bit of water.
2. Keep on heat until it turns a golden brown color, pour it into a dry pudding mold (slightly heated), and spread evenly over the inner surface.
3. Beat eggs with sugar until the sugar dissolves. While stirring, add hot milk.
4. Pour the mixture into a bowl and drizzle with nutmeg, and then cover with greased baking paper.
5. Pour 6.8 fl. oz. (200 ml) of water in the pressure cooker then put the inset on the bottom, and put the mold on it.
6. Close the pressure cooker and bring it to its full power boiling over high heat.
7. Reduce heat to low and cook for eight minutes.
8. Remove the pressure cooker from the heat and leave to cool slowly.
9. Open, remove the paper, put an inverted plate on the mold, turn it upside down, and shake gently to take the cream out.
10. Tastes great either chilled or warm.

Kher

Serves: 4

Cooking time: 25 minutes

Ingredients:

- 33.8 oz. (1 l) milk
- 2.1 oz (60 g) rice, rinsed, soaked for 2 hours and drained
- 3.5 oz. (100 g) khoya, condensed unsweetened milk (or ricotta)
- 4 tbsp. sugar
- 1 teaspoon cardamom powder
- 8 almonds, peeled and chopped

Directions:

1. In the pressure cooker, bring milk to boil, add rice, and stir. Close the pressure cooker and it bring it to full power, boiling over high heat.
2. Reduce heat to low and cook for 12 minutes.
3. Remove the pressure cooker from the heat and leave to cool slowly.
4. Open, add *khoya* and sugar, cook for about five-to-seven minutes.
5. Serve drizzled with cardamom and almonds.

A'la Apple Cake Bread Dessert
Serves: 2

Cooking time: 30 minutes

Ingredients:

- 8.8 oz. (250 g) stale bread loafs
- 1/2 cube butter
- 1/2 cup water
- 1/2 cup sugar
- 2 tbsp. rum
- 17.6 oz. (500 g)apples, peeled, with cores removed, sliced

Directions:

1. Grease the not-perforated inset with butter and arrange bread loafs on it; cover the bread with apple slices, drizzle with sugar and tiny bits of butter, then place the next layer of bread, apples etc. until you run out of the ingredients.

2. Press well and then drizzle with water and rum. Cover with a piece of baking paper and then with a tiny plate.

3. Put the inset to the pressure cooker and place it at a certain height from the bottom, using, for example, a stand.

4. Pour two cups water at the bottom of the pressure cooker, close the pressure cooker, and cook for 25 minutes from the moment you cross the threshold of the internal pressure.

5. Serve warm.

Sweet Potato in Lavender & Honey Sauce

Serves: 2

Cooking time: 12 minutes

Ingredients:

- 1 sweet potato, peeled, cut lengthwise, and then into 0.2 inch (5 cm) slices
- 3 teaspoons flower honey or other delicate honey
- 3 teaspoons dried lavender flowers
- 100 ml thick 30% cream or plant cream if its fat enough
- lemon juice
- 6.8 fl. oz. (200 ml) cold water

Directions:

1. Pour water to the pressure cooker, add sweet potato slices, honey, and lavender flowers; bring to full power and cook for 30 seconds.
2. Once ready, remove the slices with a slotted spoon.
3. Put it in the pressure cooker with the remaining residue broth on a flame and cook uncovered until the sauce thickens, if necessary, season to taste with honey.
4. Strain the broth through a sieve.
5. Add cream to the sieved broth and cook for about five more minutes until it thickens a little bit.
6. By the end, throw in a pinch of lavender flowers to enhance the intensity of flavor.
7. Pour the sauce on the potatoes.
8. Sprinkle everything with lemon juice and mix.
9. Serve either warm or chilled.

Quinoa and Red Rice Pies

Serves: 5

Cooking time: 8 minutes

Ingredients:

Licorice – strawberry sauce:

- 7 large and fresh strawberries, cut in halves lengthwise
- 1 teaspoon of licorice root powder
- 1 ½ teaspoon cocoa
- 1 tbsp. fine sugar
- 100ml water

Pies:

- 7 tbsp. quinoa, cooked (about 8-9 minutes in pressure cooker on max. pressure power)
- 4 tbsp. red rice, cooked (about 20 minutes in pressure cooker on max. pressure power)
- 2-3 strawberries per portion, cut into thin slices
- clarified butter or olive oil with butter

Directions (sauce):

1. In a pressure cooker, fry strawberry halves with sugar - without fat for a moment.
2. Once they let out a little bit of juices, add water, licorice, and cook for one minute and 40 seconds on a maximum pressure.
3. Once done, mix in the blender.
4. Wipe mixed sauce through a sieve.
5. Once again, pour the sauce to the pressure cooker and cook on high heat (with no cover), until the sauce thickens.

106

6. At the end, add cocoa and mix with a whisk to make the sauce deliciously smooth.

Directions (pies):

1. Mix rice and quinoa in a blender until totally mixed.
2. From the resulting mixture form pies of the same size and thickness.
3. Fry pies on clarified butter or olive oil with butter.

Serving: Pour one drop of sauce on a plate, and place the first pie on it (it will stick to the plate), smear it with sauce and top with strawberries cut into slices. Then, put a second pie on the strawberries and drizzle it with sauce. Garnish the top with more strawberries. You can also garnish the plate with splatters of sauce and more strawberries or other fresh red fruits.

Quinoa Pudding with Strawberry Sauce

Serves: 2

Cooking time: 15 minutes

Ingredients:

- 8 tbsp. boiled quinoa
- 17 fl. oz. (500 ml) soy milk or cow milk, preferably whole
- 2 fresh strawberries to garnish – remove stems and slice or cube
- Green cardamom – optionally, to taste (I like to add a lot, it makes the taste so great!)
- brown sugar – to taste

Directions:

1. Prepare homemade strawberry sauce (page 114)
2. Mix quinoa in a blender/food processor into a smooth mass and put into a pot.
3. In another pot, mix milk with sugar and seasonings. Cook uncovered on a low heat for about 10 minutes until the milk is aromatized.
4. Put the pot with quinoa on a heat; when the pot gets warm, start gradually adding milk, while constantly stirring with a whisk (the quinoa will get pudding-like consistency).
5. Taste and if necessary, season to your taste.
6. Serve with strawberry sauce and strawberries. Enjoy!

Bonus Section: Sauces and Bouillons

Court Bouillon
Serves: 2-3

Cooking time: 15 minutes

Ingredients:

- 1 medium carrot, sliced
- 1 medium onion, sliced
- 1 bunch of parsley, chopped
- 1 bay leaf
- 4 peppercorns
- 1 sprig of thyme
- 2.5 fl oz. (75 ml) vinegar
- salt to taste

Directions:

1. Pour 17 fl. oz. (500 ml) water into the pressure cooker; add vegetables, vinegar, and spices.
2. Close the pressure cooker and bring it to its full cooking power over high heat.
3. Reduce heat to a medium and cook for 15 minutes. Remove the pressure cooker from heat and let cool slowly.
4. Strain the broth.

White Sauce
Serves: 2

Cooking time: 10 minutes

Ingredients:

- 1 oz (30 g) flour
- 1 oz (30 g) butter
- 10 fl. oz. (300 ml) milk
- Salt and pepper to taste

Directions:

1. Melt butter in a saucepan. While stirring, gradually, add the flour and then heat for three minutes, while making sure that the mixture doesn't get browned.
2. Remove from heat and gradually pour in heated milk not to create lumps. The mixture has to be smooth.
3. Put on heat, add salt and pepper, and bring to boil while still stirring.
4. Cook for 5 minutes and keep stirring.
5. Thanks to cooking, the flavor of flour will disappear.
6. For meat dishes, you can use 50:50 milk and meat broth, for fish 50:50 milk and fish broth, for vegetables 50:50 milk and vegetable broth and for desserts milk alone or mixed with water.

Vegetable Bouillon
Serves: 4

Cooking time: 15 minutes

Ingredients:

- 1 tbsp. butter
- 1 medium onion, chopped
- 1 medium carrot, chopped
- 1 medium turnip, diced
- 2 stalks celery with leaves, coarsely chopped
- 3 sprigs of parsley
- 10 shelled pea pods
- 1.6 oz (45 g) potato peals
- 1 bay leaf
- 1 garlic clove
- 2 teaspoons of salt
- 1 teaspoon dried thyme
- 4 peppercorns
- 6 cups water

Directions:

1. Melt butter in the pressure cooker. Add all the remaining ingredients excluding salt, thyme, pepper, and water.
2. Fry until the vegetables are browned (about 5 minutes). Add all of the remaining ingredients, while stirring.
3. Close the pressure cooker and bring it to its full cooking power on high heat.
4. Reduce the heat and cook for 15 minutes.

5. Remove the pressure cooker from the fire and leave it to cool down slowly.

6. Open the pressure cooker and strain the broth through a fine sieve.

Jus-Lie Sauce
Serves: 4

Cooking time: 60 minutes

Ingredients:

- 3.5 oz. (100 g) chicken bones and offals
- 2 celery stalks
- 1 medium onion
- 1 medium carrot
- 1 bay leaf
- A pinch of thyme
- 1 teaspoon tomato passata
- 1 tbsp. corn starch
- 1 oz. (30 g) mushrooms (e.g. Champignons)
- 1 tbsp. oil
- <u>17 fl. oz. (500 ml) vegetable bouillon</u> (page 11)
- Salt and pepper

Directions:

1. Preheat the oil in the pressure cooker and brown chicken bones. Add offal, chopped vegetables, and spices and then fry them until they browned nicely.
2. Then add tomato passata and bouillon.
3. Close the pressure cooker and bring it to its full cooking power over high heat.
4. Reduce the heat to a minimum and cook for 40 minutes.
5. Remove the pressure cooker from the fire and leave to cool slowly.

6. Open the pressure cooker, remove the bones, and add cornstarch mixed with a little bit of cold water. Cook and stir, while bring it to a boil again.

7. Cook on small heat for 10-15 minutes. Mix to a smooth sauce in a blender.

Homemade Strawberry Sauce
Serves: 2
Cooking time: 5 minutes

Ingredients:

- 12 large strawberries, remove the stems, cut lengthwise in halves
- 5.4 fl. oz. (160 ml) cold water
- 2 tbsp. finely ground sugar
- 1.7 fl. oz. (50 ml) cognac/rum or other high percentage alcohol to your taste – optionally

Directions:

1. Put strawberries into preheat pressure cooker, add sugar, and stir for a while until the juice starts getting out of strawberries.
2. When the syrup starts boiling, remove it from the heat; add alcohol and flambé (cover with alcohol and set it alight briefly).
3. After 30 seconds kill the flame with a pot cover, add water and cook for about two minutes on the maximum cooking power.
4. Once ready, pour the resulting compote into a blender and mix well.
5. Run the compote through a sieve and pour into the pot again.
6. Stir the mixture in the pot set over a high heat until the sauce gets thicker.
7. Serve warm or cold.

Recommended Reading For You:

Gluten-Free Vegan Cookbook: 90+ Healthy, Easy and Delicious Recipes for Vegan Breakfasts, Salads, Soups, Lunches, Dinners and Desserts

90+ Healthy, Easy and Delicious Recipes for Vegan Breakfasts, Salads, Soups, Lunches, Dinners and Desserts for Your Well-Being + Shopping List to Save Your Precious Time!

Gluten-Free Vegan diet doesn't have to be bland and boring at all! These recipes are original, easy to make and just delightfully appetizing. They will enrich your culinary experience and let you enjoy your breakfasts, lunches, dinners and desserts with your friends and family.

In this book you will find:

-23 Scrumptious and Easy Breakfasts

-27 Delicious and Savory Lunches and Dinners

-22 Aromatic And Nutritious Soups

-21 Enticing And Rich Desserts

-Extra Shopping List to Save Your Precious Time

= 93 Fantastic Gluten-Free Healthy Vegan Recipes!

The Gluten-Free diet will help you detoxify, improve your immune system and make you feel younger - both mentally and physically! The Change is just in front of you!

->**Direct Buy Link:** http://www.amazon.com/dp/B00LU915YA/

->**Paperback Version:** https://www.createspace.com/4907669

Fast Freezer Meals: 46 Delicious and Quick Gluten-Free Slow Cooker Recipes for Make-Ahead Meals That Will Save Your Time and Improve Your Health

Discover Delicious and Quick Gluten-Free Slow Cooker Recipes for Make-Ahead Meals That Will Save Your Time and Improve Your Health!

As a busy businesswoman, wife and mom I know exactly how hard it is to prepare healthy and tasty meals for me and my family every day, especially when they have to be gluten-free! See yourself that gluten-diet doesn't have to be bland, and **home cooking doesn't have to be time-consuming! Most of these recipes can be prepared in no more than 30 minutes and then just effortlessly cooked in your crockpot when you're at work or doing your business!**

-I included a shopping list inside to save your precious time.

-No matter if you are gluten intolerant or not – these meals are delicious, healthy and suitable for everyone!

-In this book you will also find freezing and thawing safety guide.

These recipes will enrich your culinary experience and let you save massive time!

->**Direct Buy Link:** http://www.amazon.com/dp/B00M783PS2/

->**Paperback Version:** https://www.createspace.com/4944068

Paleo Smoothie Recipes: 67 Delicious Paleo Smoothies for Weight Loss and a Healthy Lifestyle

67 Easy and Fast Delicious Smoothie Recipes for Effective Weight Loss and Sexy Body!

Kill the food cravings and get in shape with these delicious and healthy Paleo Smoothies!

In This Book I'll Show You:

-Why Paleo Smoothies are great for Weight Loss (and Weight Maintenance!)

-67 Tasty Paleo Recipes great for Weight Loss, Detox, and keeping your body Healthy every day!

-How to make the Paleo approach easier!

-Important facts about some of the ingredients you'd like to know.

-Planning and Directions – how to get started fast!

-How to maintain your motivation, finally lose the extra pounds and be happy with a Sexy Body!

->**Direct Buy Link:** http://www.amazon.com/dp/B00J8ZHMIQ/

->**Paperback Version:** https://www.createspace.com/4803901

Gluten Free Crock Pot Recipes: 59 Healthy, Easy and Delicious Slow Cooker Paleo Recipes for Breakfast, Lunch and Dinner

Discover Healthy, Easy and Delicious Slow Cooker Paleo Recipes for Breakfast, Lunch and Dinner for You and Your Family!

Save your time and start healthy living with these delectable slow cooker gluten free recipes tailor-made for busy people!

I've been on the Gluten Free diet for more than ten years now! Although the main reason for my radical diet change was my diagnosis (Coeliac disease), I would never-ever (even if given a magical chance) take the lane of eating gluten again!

->**Direct Buy Link:** http://www.amazon.com/dp/B00K5UVYUA/

->**Paperback Version:** https://www.createspace.com/4823966

Low Carb Slow Cooker: 50 Delicious, Fast and Easy Crock Pot Recipes for Rapid Weight Loss

Start Losing Weight Effectively and For Good!

The recipes mentioned in this eBook are not only simple but they require every day ingredients from your kitchen.
Food tastes best when you cook it with some love.
Nothing can beat the mouth-watering dishes that can be cooked in a slow cooker.
If you often find yourself confused about how to whip up a yummy dish for a low-carb diet, this eBook is just the perfect thing you need right now.

In This Book You Will Read About:

-What is Low Carb Diet?
-Who Should Use it And Who Should Not?
-Pros and Properties of Low Carb Diet
-Some Common Low Carb Myths
-Best and Worst Food Choices You Can Make
-Foods You Need to Avoid
-Important Tips and Advice
-10 Low-Carb Slow-Cooker Aromatic Soups Recipes
-11 Low-Carb Crockpot Delicious Chicken recipes
-10 Low-carb Slow-cooker Amazingly Good Sea-food
-10 Low-carb slow-cooker Yummy Pork Recipes
-9 Low-carb Slow-cooker Scrumptious Lamb Recipes

->**Direct Buy Link:** http://www.amazon.com/dp/B00O2AACR0/

->**Paperback Version:** https://www.createspace.com/5042178

Anti-Inflammatory Diet: Beginner's Guide: What You Need To Know To Heal Yourself with Food + Recipes + One Week Diet Plan

"He who takes medicine and neglects to diet wastes the skill of his doctors." - *Chinese Proverb*

Are you suffering from the severe symptoms that you've been trying to overcome for a long time now using your prescribed pills, but just stuck somewhere in the middle?

Unrestrained inflammation lead to asthma, allergies, tissue and cell degeneration, heart diseases, cancer and various other maladies, which are difficult to deal with.
I myself suffered from long and gruesome periods of acute inflammation. I had the IBS symptoms and very bad, extremely painful sinusitis. It started to affect my day to day ability to work and my potential and productivity suffered a steep decline. Medication helped but the effect was only temporary. I would be confined to my house for days without any solution to my problem. Every doctor I visited could pinpoint the superficial problem and treat it but none could tell me what was causing this problem, time after time.

And the problem was my diet!
Vast majority of the recipes I included in this book can be prepared really fast and easily! I also included absolutely delicious One Week Diet Plan for you!

->**Direct Buy Link:** http://www.amazon.com/dp/B00MQ9HI58/

->**Paperback Version:** https://www.createspace.com/4974692

You may also want to download my friend's books. Help your mind today with these:

- Buddhism: Beginner's Guide:

http://www.amazon.com/dp/B00MHSR5YM/

- Meditation: Beginner's Guide:

http://www.amazon.com/ dp/B00KQRU9BC/

- Zen: Beginner's Guide:

http://www.amazon.com/dp/B00PWUBSEK/

My Mailing List: If you would like to **receive new Kindle reads** on **weight loss, wellness, diets, recipes and healthy living** for **FREE** I invite you to my Mailing List. Whenever my new book is out, I set the free period for two days. You will get an e-mail notification and will **be the first to get the book for $0** during its limited promotion.

Why would I do this when it took me countless hours to write these e-books?

First of all, that's my way of saying **"thank you"** to my new readers. Second of all – **I want to spread the word about my new books and ideas.** Mind you that **I hate spam and e-mails that come too frequently** - no worries about that.

If you think that's a good idea and are in, just follow this link:

http://eepurl.com/6elQD

You can also follow us on Facebook:

www.facebook.com/HolisticWellnessBooks

We have created this page with a few fellow authors of mine. We hope you find it inspiring and helpful.

Thank You for your time and interest in our work!

Annette Goodman & Holistic Wellness eBooks

About The Author

Hello! My name is Annette Goodman.

I'm glad we met. Who am I?

A homegrown cook, successful wellness aficionado and a writer. I live in Portland, Oregon with my husband, son and our dear golden retriever, Fluffy. I work as a retail manager in of the European companies.

My entire childhood I suffered from obesity, hypertension and complexion problems. During my college years I decided to turn my life around and started my weight-loss and wellness pursue. After more than a decade I can say that I definitely succeeded and now I'd like to give you a hand.

I love creating new healthy recipes, cooking and writing books about healthy lifestyle for you to enjoy and profit from.

I hope we'll meet again!

My Amazon author page:

http://www.amazon.com/Annette-Goodman/e/B00LLPE1QM/ref=ntt_athr_dp_pel_1